All About WHALES!

A SEA WORLD BOOK ™

Published by

THIRD STORY BOOKS™
955 Connecticut Avenue, Suite 1302
Bridgeport, Connecticut 06607

ISBN 1-884506-08-9

Distributed to the trade by
Andrews & McMeel
4900 Main Street
Kansas City, Missouri 64112

Library of Congress Catalog Card Number: 93-61827

All photographs used courtesy of Sea World,
except the following:
Mark Conlin: 10, 11 bottom, 15 bottom
Howard Hall: 7 bottom, 9, 12, 13, 15 top

Printed in Singapore

All About WHALES!

Written by Deborah Kovacs

FEATURING *SeaWorld.* PHOTOGRAPHY

THIRD™
STORY
BOOKS

What is a Whale?

Some people think that because whales live in water, they are fish.

But whales are mammals, like dogs, bears…and people. Like all mammals, whales have warm blood. Like us, they breathe through their lungs and give birth to live young. Newborn whales even have a few hairs!

The gray whale was hunted almost to extinction as late as the 1930s, but thanks to greater conservation efforts, today there are over 21,000 in existence.

The earliest known ancestors of whales were four-legged creatures that lived on land about 55 million years ago.

As these creatures changed over millions of years, they went to live in the water. Their back legs disappeared, and their forelegs became flippers. Their nostrils moved to the top of their heads. They gained blubber, the layer of fat that keeps them warm in cold water.

Whales have different communication techniques, and although humans can't talk to whales, they can communicate in different ways.

Healthy adult killer whales roam the oceans without fear from other predators, yet they still face the challenges of living in the wild.

More About Whales

Whales can't breathe through their mouths like we can. When a whale needs air, it surfaces and takes in a deep breath from a blowhole located on top of its head. Before it takes in air, it blows a spout of water vapor out of the blowhole.

Sometimes whales hunt for food by a process known as echolocation. They send out sounds which bounce off of, or echo, objects. The whale then determines what that object is from the sound of the echo.

Killer whales, like all whales, have blowholes on the top of their heads. They also have dorsal fins.

Whales have flippers, which they use for steering. Their tails are made up of two lobes called flukes. The powerful tail flukes move up and down for swimming. Some whales have a dorsal fin, which they use for balance.

Whales steer with their flippers and propel themselves through water by moving their powerful tail flukes up and down.

The eye of a Southern right whale.

Where Do Whales Live?

Killer whales can appear almost any time, in most waters of the world.

Whales live in all the world's oceans. Some whales travel thousands of miles each year, migrating between colder waters, where they feed, and warmer waters, where they raise their young. Other whales stay close to the colder waters of the Arctic and Antarctic.

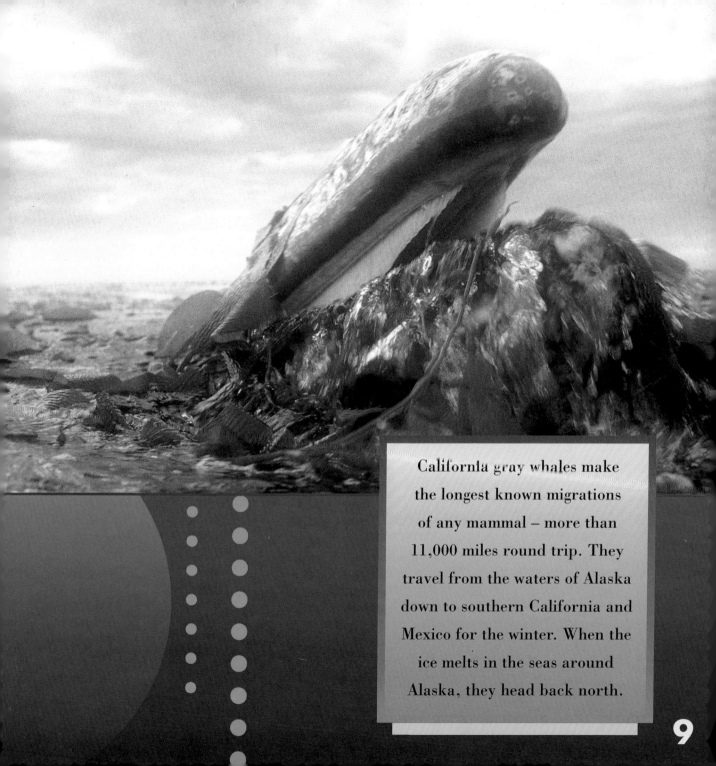

California gray whales make the longest known migrations of any mammal – more than 11,000 miles round trip. They travel from the waters of Alaska down to southern California and Mexico for the winter. When the ice melts in the seas around Alaska, they head back north.

Little, Bigger, Biggest

There are more than 76 different kinds of whales. The biggest whale is the blue whale, which may be more than 90 feet long. It is the biggest living animal on earth. The smallest whales are porpoises, which are usually about four to six feet long.

The front part of the blue whale, the largest mammal on earth.

The killer whale is the best-known whale at Sea World. These black-and-white mammals can grow to be 26 feet long and can weigh more than 12,000 pounds. Killer whales can be found in all oceans of the world, especially in the colder waters of the Arctic or Antarctic.

The black-and-white colors of the killer whale can make it hard for fish to see the whale under water.

The dolphin is one of the smallest of all whales.

A humpback whale.

Humpback whales are famous because they seem to "sing." The sounds that humpback whales make are called "songs." A humpback whale's song can last as long as 30 minutes. Humpbacks have very long pectoral flippers, and their heads, flippers and tail flukes are usually covered with barnacles.

Gray whales are medium-sized, growing to as long as 45 feet. Because they travel close to shore when migrating south, they can easily be seen from the shores of the western United States.

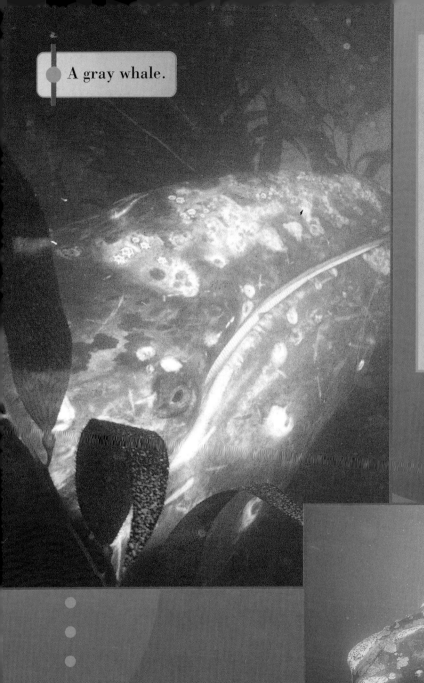

A gray whale.

The plumpest whales are right whales. They have no dorsal fin and are slow swimmers. Right whales are easily recognizable by the hard, crusty areas of skin that form on their heads.

A Southern right whale.

How Do Whales Eat?

Those whales that have teeth are called toothed whales, but they still don't chew their food. The teeth are designed for gripping their food rather than chewing. They swallow their food whole or in very large chunks. Most toothed whales eat fish.

Baleen whales are called "mysticetes." Mysticete means "whale with mustache."

A toothed whale's teeth are not necessarily sharp. It uses its teeth to grip food, not chew it.

A gray whale uses baleen to catch food.

Whales without teeth are called baleen whales. They have hairy-edged plates in their mouths, called baleen. Baleen is like a filter. To eat, baleen whales take in huge gulps of sea water. They press out the sea water through their baleen plates and food gets trapped.

A blue whale feeds on krill. A blue whale is a baleen whale.

15

Whale Babies

A baby killer whale is born head first.

Whale babies (calves) are born underwater. Sometimes they are born head first, sometimes tail first. When a killer whale is born, it is usually between seven and eight feet long, weighing about 300 pounds. Whale babies drink their mother's milk, just like any other mammal. Whales usually begin nursing several hours after they are born.

Whale calves stay close by their mothers for a year or more. Sometimes a mother whale helps her calf swim by creating a current, called a slipstream, that the calf can ride in.

This little killer whale is being born tail first.

A calf catches a ride in its mother's slipstream.

Whale Behavior

When a whale slaps its tail flukes
against the surface of the water,
it is called *lobtailing*.
A whale *breaches* when it jumps
out of the water.
When a whale breathes through its
blowhole at the surface of the water
and sends up a spray of water vapor,
it is *spouting*.
A whale that sticks its head straight up
out of the water is *spyhopping*.

Breaching.

Spyhopping.

The first step in lobtailing.

Because whales spend most of their lives under water, almost everything a whale does in the wild is a mystery to us. But from time to time, whales come to the surface. Then, some of their behaviors can be seen. Sea World allows us to study the underwater behavior of whales.

Are Whales Endangered?

Once, whales roamed the oceans in greater numbers than they do today. But whales have been hunted in great numbers, for their meat and for their blubber, melted to make oil. Many, but not all, species of whales are endangered. Some, like the Northern right whales, are almost extinct. Today, most whale hunting is against the law. Endangered whale species are slowly, slowly coming back. Still, pollution and traffic in the seas are also big dangers for whales.

The pictures on these pages show, in part, how whales are brought back to sea. This Bryde's whale was rescued, nursed back to health and then carefully transported from its pool at Sea World to a boat to be returned to its native habitat.

Whales and People

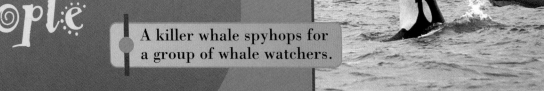

A killer whale spyhops for a group of whale watchers.

Many people are excited to see whales. Some people get to see whales in the wild, by going on a whale-watch. Other people visit whales in oceanaria, like Sea World. The more we learn about whales, the more we can help make sure that they will live on, in great numbers.

Whales usually enjoy their contact with humans. Whales are social animals and enjoy learning and exercising.

A degree in oceanography could get you up close and personal with a whale.

Even without a degree, you can still get close to a whale.

Whales enjoy the company of other whales.

23

Whales and Sea World

Shamu swims up on a platform to interact with his trainer.

Not as much is known as we would like about whales because so much of their time is spent under the water, far away from land. Organizations like Sea World help us learn more about what whales need to survive and flourish, both in the wild and in the care of humans. Much of what we know about these wondrous creatures we have learned from organizations such as Sea World.

Sea World is home to many killer whales, as well as other kinds of whales such as the beluga whale, the false killer whale, and the pilot whale.

One of the great effects of training whales is that it is possible to train them for husbandry purposes. A whale can do a rocket hop or can lay still on its back so that blood samples can be taken.

The popular rocket hop.

These whales have been trained to lie on their backs while blood is drawn for analysis.

25

A trainer communicates with a whale by means of a computer system.

This beached pygmy sperm whale calf will be hand-fed until it is well enough to eat on its own.

A beached whale is given treatment for an infection.

Whales at Sea World help researchers and the public learn about many things, including whale behavior, whale communication, how whales are born, and how mother whales care for their young.

A number of public-interest groups and individuals are involved with whale conservation. Researchers and scientists study whales all over the world.

This whale is given help in keeping right-side-up. Sometimes beached whales need help in adjusting to a new environment.

Fascinating Facts

Zoom. Toothed whales are fast swimmers. Really fast. There are records of toothed whales swimming as fast as 22 miles per hour for short spurts.

Way Down Under. Whales can dive deeply. Sperm whales can dive deeper than 3,000 feet.

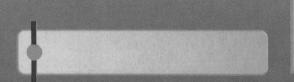

Gulp! Some baleen whales can take in 150 pounds of fish and plankton at a time. They may eat as much as one ton of food a day. That's two thousand boxes of cereal!

Hold Your Breath. Some kinds of whales can stay under water, without coming up for air, for as long as an hour-and-a-half.

What's That, You Say? Whale sounds carry very far under water. Nobody knows just how far, but it's possible that these sounds travel, and may be heard, many, many miles away.

Whozat? The flukes of each humpback whale are as individual as fingerprints. Researchers who study certain populations of humpbacks in the wild can tell the difference between one humpback and another by studying its tail flukes. They even give these whales names, according to designs they see on the flukes. (For example, one whale, missing a piece of a fluke, is called Notch; another with speckles on its flukes is called Pepper.)

Spouting Off. Each kind of whale makes a certain-shaped spout. Trained observers can see the spout of a whale at a distance, and can say what kind of whale it is.

Sing, Sing a Song. Beluga whales are sometimes called "canaries of the sea" because of the high-pitched, chirping sounds they make.

Glossary

Baleen Fringed plates that hang inside the mouths of baleen whales. The fringes on baleen plates hold on to tiny plants, fish and animals (organisms) eaten by baleen whales.

Blubber This thick layer of fat lies under the skin of whales and keeps them warm in icy ocean water.

Blowhole Opening to the lungs of a whale, similar to human nostrils.

Breaching When a whale jumps clear out of the water, it is said to breach.

Echolocation Toothed whales make clicking sounds and listen for the echo of these sounds. The echo tells the whale the size, shape, and distance of objects around them.

Endangered An endangered species is anything or anyone whose continued existence is threatened.

Flukes Flukes are lobes that make up the whale's tail. A whale pushes itself through the water by pushing its flukes up and down.

Herd Several pods of whales.

Husbandry Careful management of resources.

Hydrophone An underwater microphone used by researchers.

Krill Tiny shrimp-like animals that make up the main diet of some baleen whales.

Lobtailing When a whale slaps its flukes against the surface of the water, it is lobtailing.

Migrate To travel from one home to another home. Some whales migrate many thousands of miles each year.

Pod A group of whales. When several pods of whales come together it is called a herd.

Predator An animal that eats other animals.

Rocket Hop A performance at Sea World where a whale shoots straight out of the water with a trainer on his nose. At the height of the whale's breach, the trainer dives off.

Slipstream A current that a whale creates as it swims. Sometimes a mother whale creates a slipstream for her calf to swim in.

Spout When a whale breathes out at the surface, droplets of water mix with the outgoing air. The resulting vapor spray is called a spout. Different types of whales make differently-shaped spouts.

Spyhopping When a whale pokes its head straight up above the surface of the water, it is spyhopping. Whales may spyhop as a way to look at what's going on above the surface.

Sea World®

"For in the end we will conserve only what we love.
We will love only what we understand.
And we will understand only what we are taught."
Baba Dioum — noted Central African Naturalist

Since the first Sea World opened in 1964, more than 160 million people have experienced first-hand the majesty and mystery of marine life. Sea World parks have been leaders in building public understanding and appreciation for killer whales, dolphins, and a vast variety of other sea creatures.

Through its work in animal rescue and rehabilitation, breeding, animal care, research and education, Sea World demonstrates a strong commitment to the preservation of marine life and the environment.

Sea World provides all its animals with the highest-quality care including state-of-the-art facilities and stimulating positive reinforcement training programs. Each park employs full-time veterinarians, trainers, biologists and other animal care experts to provide 24-hour care. Through close relationships with these animals — relationships that are built on trust — Sea World's animal care experts are able to monitor their health every day to ensure their well being. In short, all animals residing at Sea World are treated with respect, love and care.

If you would like more information about Sea World books, please write to us. We'd like to hear from you.

THIRD STORY BOOKS
955 Connecticut Avenue, Suite 1302
Bridgeport, CT 06607